Clouds
are the Dust of
HIS FEET

Ruth Bell Graham

Clouds are the Dust of HIS FEET

Crossway Books

Acknowledgments

Steve Griffith is what I would call a motivator, an inspirer. Because of him this little volume of "Clouds" came to be.

I owe my warmest thanks to Luci Shaw, a <u>true</u> poet, and one whom I have admired for years. Steve persuaded her to go over my attempts to clarify, simplify and beautify them. To Luci, I am deeply, deeply indebted. And for her foreword, words are inadequate to express my appreciation.

And always, I am indebted to my secretary, Evelyn Freeland, who has done all my typing over and over again with never a word of complaint.

Then, too, a word of special appreciation for those who inspired certain poems.

Glimpses into a Soul

I suppose everyone, at some time in their lives, in some creative moment of romance or experience or emotion, gives birth to a poem. Poems embody life in a way that is as different from prose as singing or whistling is from speaking, or dancing is from a business-like walk. Some people continue to write verse, to make it a part of their ongoing experience. But very few keep and polish their poetry long enough to allow it to represent *them*—to form a body of work that shows the unique, lovely growth of an individual from youth to maturity.

Ruth Bell Graham is one who has given us such a body of work, as represented both in her earlier book of verse, *Sitting by My Laughing Fire*, and in the volume you hold in your hand. In both of them she shows us her inner self, over nearly a lifetime, in an intensely personal, appealing way.

The author of this book is a word-weaver, with an instinctive, unaffected poetic skill. Her writing shows us a series of candid pictures of her own life—growing up in China, as a young girl in a missionary school in North Korea, a college student, a bride, a wife and homemaker, a mother, and a woman of God who graciously carries His presence into the public arena. She shows herself to be an adventurer, a first-hand observer of storm and shore and sea, of birdsong and meadow and tree, alert to both rain and sunshine and the nuances of seasons. An avid learner, a worshiper, she's a lover of people and a friend of God.

Poetry is a redemptive act. Poets are little creators, translating life into art, the seasons of struggle and choice in metaphors that illustrate with a kind of primal reality and vigor. Each separate poem in this book is a little memorial to some moment of truth, some gleam of light, some wrench of the heart or leap of the imagination. The most "ordinary" incidents, in poems, turn extraordinary; the visible world is enlarged, charged with the numinous—the unseen real, the *supernatural*; heaven is glimpsed here on earth. In her poetry Ruth Graham practices *incarnational theology* because God's truth is enfleshed in her human experience. When it flows so naturally, yet deliberately, from an authentic spirit, it is a beautiful thing to see.

I feel as though I have moved through the windows of these poems into a soul where God lives. You will, too.

Luci Shaw

Clouds are the dust of His Feet
and watching the evening sky
I chuckled to think, "How neat.
God just passed by."

Not Yours, but You

It isn't your gold or silver,
your talents great or small,
your voice, or your gift of drawing,
or the crowd you go with at all;
it isn't your friends or pastimes,
your looks or your clothes so gay;
it isn't your home or family,
or even the things that you say;
it isn't your choice of amusements,
it isn't the life you lead,
it isn't the thing you prize the most,
or the books you like to read;
no, it isn't the things you have, dear,
or the things you like to do,
the Master is searching deeper . . .
He seeks not yours, but *you*.

It's your heart that Jesus longs for;
your will to be made His own,
with self on the cross forever,
and Jesus alone on the throne.

Tsingkiangpu, N. Kiangsu, China, 1934

Inasmuch

"Inasmuch" a cup of water
    offered one in Jesus' name,
"Inasmuch" a gentle handclasp
    treating one and all the same,
"Inasmuch" a single penny
    dropped in some poor beggar's palm,
"Inasmuch" a piece of clothing
    just to keep a body warm,
"Inasmuch," so said the Master
    (though the very least he be),
"Inasmuch as done to someone
    you have done it unto Me."

Pyeng Yang Foreign School (Sophomore Year),
Korea, 1934

Doxology

Now unto Him Who is able
   spotless to keep His own,
presenting each ransomed sinner
   blameless before the throne,
to the only wise God, our Father,
   to Him Whom we all adore,
be glory, dominion, and power
   both now and forevermore.

Pyeng Yang, Korea, 1934-1935

Gift

Lord Jesus, take this life of mine,
    worthless as it may be,
cleanse it, and fill it, and make it shine,
    that it may be bright for Thee.

Pyeng Yang Foreign School, Korea, 1935

So Brief

Like a shadow declining
    swiftly away, away,
like the dew of the morning
    gone with the heat of the day;
like a wind in the treetops,
    like a wave of the sea,
so are our lives on earth when seen
    in the light of eternity.

Pyeng Yang, Korea, Spring, 1937

Spare Not the Pain

Spare not the pain
though the way I take
   be lonely and dark,
though the whole soul ache,
   for the flesh must die
though the heart may break.
   Spare not the pain, oh,
     spare not the pain.

Fall of 1937, before leaving China for college

Knowing Jesus

When we come to know Jesus as Savior
and accept Him as Master as well,
He is more than anyone told us,
and more than we ever can tell.

1938

Only You

Dusty my soul tonight.
Earth has been dear.
Bewildered, I come to You,
Father God, hear.
Idols that charm me,
dreams that allure,
pains that alarm me,
suspense to endure,
memories that linger,
thoughts that ensnare,
a heart that is aching,
all crumpled by care,
unsatisfied, restless,
scarce able to pray—
everything, everything
take it away.

Only You,
none but You,
Jesus alone:
ashes the rest to me,
songs with a groan,
take them each one away—
mind not my tears—
lift me above this earth's
joys and its fears,
give me Yourself alone—
nothing beside—
so will I be with You,
content,
satisfied!

College, 1939

Exodus 14:14

"The Lord shall fight for you, and you
shall hold your peace."
Look up, O you of little faith;
let doubting cease.
The battle is the Lord's; He works
in a mysterious way.
'Tis not by might, nor power, but see
His spirit move today.
Unprofitable servants we;
our duty done, we must
watch for His victory,
so, fearful one,
be still, and trust.

Wheaton, January 8, 1939

Psalm 61:2

So helpless a thing my heart
 and, oh, so small
all overwhelmed, it looks to You for strength,
 nor looks in vain;
long it has struggled on, and now at length
 is crushed again.

Eager with expectation, rising
 only to fall,
wearily it longs for that great Rock
 "higher than I,"
where, with Your strength absorbing every shock,
 calm shall I lie.

Wheaton, Spring, 1940

Be Still

You held my hand
and I,
feeling a strange,
sweet thrill,
spoke to my heart
a sharp rebuke,
told it—
Be still.

You held me close
and I
gasped, "Oh, no!"
until
my heart within rose
and told me—
Be still.

October 24, 1942, after engagement to Bill

To Bill

There are so many thoughts on love
all carefully penned out . . .
But it was not I who wrote them, dear,
nor you they wrote about.
I wish my heart—all over-full
might add one little line.
Something expressed for only you
something that was all mine.
It would not be original,
nor one with subtle powers,
nor would it live through endless years
But dear—it would be ours.

Worthy

God, make me worthy to be his wife:
as cliffs are made, so make me strong,
a help for him when things go wrong.
Clear as the dew, Lord, make my mind,
clear as the dew, and just as kind;
and make me a refreshment, too,
a quiet encourager, like You;
I'll laugh with him in face of tears,
in face of worries and of fears;
brave to be and do and bear,
both quick to yield, and glad to share.
Remind him, God, through coming days
how warm is my love for him always.
his head's held high as he faces life;
God, make me worthy to be his wife.

November, 1941

Dreams Come True

It was so very good of God
to let my dreams come true,
to note a young girl's cherished hopes,
then lead her right to you.
So good of Him to take such care
in little, detailed parts
(He knows how much such details mean
to young and wishful hearts);
so good of Him to let you be
tall and slender, too,
with waving hair more blond than brown
and eyes of steely blue.

Wheaton, 1941

Common Things

Lord, let mine be
a common place
while I am here.
His was a common one;
He seems so near
when I am working
at some ordinary task.
Lord, let mine be
a common one, I ask.
Give me the things to do
that others shun,
I am not gifted or so poised,
Lord, as some.
I am best fitted
for the common things,
and I am happy so.
It always brings
a sense of fellowship
with Him Who learned
to do the lowly things
that others spurned:
to wear the simple clothes,
the common dress,
to gather in His arms
and gently bless
(and He was busy, too)
a little child,
to lay his hand upon
the one defiled,
to walk with sinners
down some narrow street,
to kneel Himself
and wash men's dusty feet.
To ride a common foal,
to work with wood,
to dwell with common folk,
eat common food;
and then upon the city dump
to die for me
in view of all who passed.
Lord, common things
are all I've ever asked
of Thee.

1942

Long Night

Dear one,
I was cross last night
and you had worked
so hard all day.
Quietly you said, "Good night,"
closed the door,
and went away.

Nights can be
so very long
when hearts are far
that should be near;
I cannot wait
for day to come
and hear you say
"Good morning,
Dear."

College

Wedding

I'll be a bride—
your bride, dear—
in just a day
or two.
There'll be white
and a long veil
(like mist)
to see up through.
There'll be flowers,
and music,
and after our vows,
a prayer,
and after the prayer
your firm, sweet kiss,
and people everywhere.
There will be rice in showers,
perhaps a can or two.
Distance then,
and darkness,
and then
there'll be you!

Grace

The sin-scarred
brush His white,
white robes;
the wounded
touch
His feet;
the dying
whisper
His name in prayer,
wondering sweetly
to find Him
there
where hell
and the sinner
meet.

He took of His grace,
His infinite grace,
And soldiers wondered
to find a trace
of tears
in the grime
on a dead man's face.
"The going
must've been tough,"
they said,
not knowing
that death
for a man,
forgiven by God,
is easy going.

Montreat, North Carolina, September 16, 1944
World War II with R.M.

Endless

Please, God,
let my heart kneel always,
Love its only master,
knowing the warm impulsiveness
of shattered alabaster:
I know You can see things
the way a new bride sees,
So never let it end, God,
never. Please?

Fall, 1943

Home

Ours is a little home
newly begun.
So, we would ask of Thee,
Lord, let it always be
chuck full of fun.

Homes, even newest ones,
often are full of
things unexpected, gray;
so let it be alway
bursting with love.

This, and above it all,
one special plea:
'mid outward storms, still it
and storm or calm, fill it,
Lord, full of Thee.

Hinsdale, Illinois, Fall, 1943

Hidden Heart

Now that I love you
and see with eyes
by love enlightened
and made wise,
I wonder how
men look at you
who do not see you
as I do?
They see (they must)
the fire and steel,
the driving force
I also feel.

But do they ever,
ever see
that gentler side
revealed to me?
That wealth of
tenderness
man stores
within his heart
from other men
and guards, and keeps
and then outpours
when with the woman
he adores?

Early marriage

House and Home

"Man builds; God hallows."
F.B.M.

Dear Lord,
we've built this little house
with sloping eaves, and windows wide,
gray stone walls, and rustic doors,
and paneled all inside.

We've prayed
and planned and built this house.
And here we pause, for You alone
can by Your presence hallow it
and make this house a home.

Montreat, 1947

"I have heard the prayer and plea you have made before me; I have consecrated this temple, which you have built, by putting my home there forever. My eyes and my heart will always be there." 1 Kings 9:3

Little Piney Cove

We bought this cove
when coves were cheap,
flatland scarce,
mountains steep.
Not once
were we ever told
in autumn
poplars
turn to gold.

Oh, it was cheap
(beyond belief)
but autumn makes me feel
a thief.

September 27, 1975

Puppet

Puppet,
poor puppet,
who's pulling your strings?

Puppets can't answer,
puppets just swing;
puppets hang there
empty and sweet,
kill on command
and pillage the street.

Puppet,
poor puppet,
who's pulling your strings?

1967

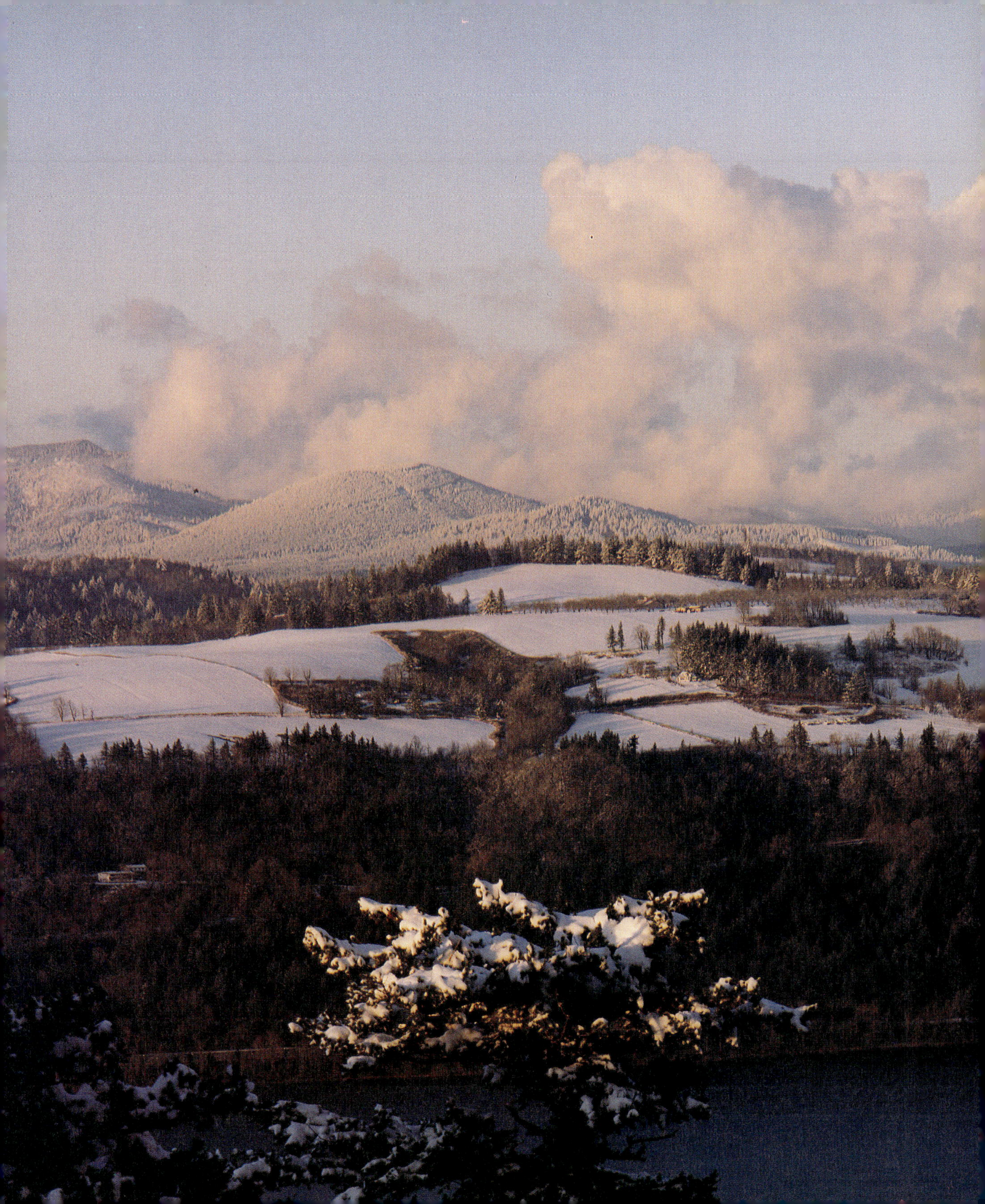

Sundown

Turbulent ocean
billowing clouds
numinous
reflecting
briefly glorified
by the westering sun
incandescent
liquid reflection
in the surf
easing out . . .
Wind in my face
and the waves sighing
moment of glory,
soul-catching,
gone.

Gulls
and sandpipers
looking for food.

Vero Beach, 1972

Ode to Emily and Charles

The night
Bill told me
he loved me,
what
did he discuss?
Us?
No.
Emily!
    Beautiful.
    Sweet.
    Talented.
    Spiritual.
    (And second cousin to
       Herbert Hoover!)
    Emily!
I got madder,
(not sadder),
just madder and madder,
till *blam*!
with a slam
we rammed
into a truck
(what luck!).

(He was so busy looking
back he couldn't see where
he was going. There's a
moral here, but we won't
belabor it.)
Still,
there were no quarrels
thanks to Charles!

I met her
years later
and knew
I would
hate her.
I hoped,
without praying
(that goes
without saying),
but I hoped
(how I hoped!)
by now
she'd become
fat and dumb.

Well?
She was a doll!
What's more,
after all,
I liked her!
She'd earned all those laurels.
Still,
Thank you, Charles!!

Thus
by the happy twists
of life
folks pair off
as man and wife,
and children come
to bless each home:

Charles
Caroline
Joyce
David
Gigi
Anne
Bunny
Franklin
Ned

This is the moral
of my ode
(if this is an ode,
and if odes have morals):
Thank you, Charles!

Little Piney Cove, November 6, 1971
Written for the first get-together of the two families

The Thief

"Punished justly, . . . getting what our deeds deserve. . . . Today, . . . with me in Paradise." Luke 23:41-43.

He died—
the thief—
and yet,
before,
he'd cried
for mercy
and, what's more,
his tortured soul
had found relief.

He got
a death
that he deserved;
a Life
that he did not.

London, September 14, 1972

Parting

This is the day
Ned left for school—
a good day for flying,
cold but clear.
Perhaps I wouldn't feel
this way
if school were near.

1972

Inauguration

Low gray skies,
clouds
moving fast,
crowds,
one man,
and a flag
half mast.

Washington, D.C.
January 20, 1973

Cemetery

Larger than life
he lived here,
smaller than death
he lies
under the spreading oak trees,
under the skies.

If mercy is for sinners,
(which God
in mercy gives)
smaller than Life
he lived here,
larger than death
he lives.

L.B.J. Ranch Cemetery
January 25, 1973

Birdsong Remembered

A burst of song
as the bird flew by,
hotly pursued
by an angry bird;
I saw,
I heard,
not knowing why,
or which was right
or wrong,
nor whence they came
nor went.
I only know
that burst of flight,
that mocking song,
is mine to keep
for merriment,
this whole day long.

Caneel Bay, Virgin Islands
February 7, 1973

Which?

If I were stranded
on the moon,
my spacecraft
disappearing in the sky,
alone in lunar vastness,
doomed to die,
would I be
frozen in alone-ness
despair
or
aware
of Thee?

Caneel Bay, Virgin Islands
February 10, 1973

Not Easy, but Precious

"Death, be not long.
Death, be not hard,"
we prayed.
But days stretched year-like
and when death came, God
it was not easy
as we had prayed.
Quiet, but not easy.

Forgive my complaints;
for precious to You
is the death of Your saints.

November, 1974

Facade

Manicured, styled,
expensively suited,
they stood
and they smiled
as if programmed, computed,
by specialists fed;
yet I knew within each
beat a heart living-dead.
The smiles were a mask;
the life-styles they led
at best a brave showing,
pretending, not being,
While You Who created
are God, the All-Knowing,
are God, the All-seeing.
Lord, we cannot see
as You see above,
behind and within. We
only can love.

Mequon, Wisconsin, May 5, 1975

White Flowers

White flowers
in memory of her,
this year—
my first.
I'd thought
they'd bring a tear,
my heart would burst.
Yet flowers brought
a flood of memories
with which
my life
is full.
Because of her
I'm rich.

Sunday May 11, 1975

Alive

May I so live,
may I so thrive,
that folks will know
I am alive.
How dreary should
my life be so
if someone asked,
and didn't *know*.

May 30, 1975

Accompanied

He does not go alone
this gangling boy, all legs and arms;
awkward, and gentle, and so prone
to sudden impulse. What alarms
mothers at home, praying, sleepless, tense,
are all the "what-ifs" Satan sends
as if in glee. And still I sense
he is accompanied, and apprehend
divine forethought, guidance and, when needed,
an Intervening Hand. So I would pray
in gratitude. And, having heeded
God's promise, I can praise today.

"Thou wilt keep him in superlative
peace whose imagination stops
at Thee." Isaiah 26:3
      Marginal Note

Europe, June 26, 1976

Empty

A house
is not the same
when she
who made it home
is gone;
it looks
as it has always
looked
and yet
forlorn.
There is an emptiness
within,
a silence
where her chuckle was.
From now on
it is me alone
who once was "us."

September 8, 1976

Concern and Confidence

They say
I must not care so much,
or feel so deeply.
I shouldn't study
or read depressing books
like *Under the Rubble*,
or *China Today*.
Rather, I should play,
read Agatha Christie,
and relax.
Which would mean
bottling up my
deepest concerns,
turning off my mind,
and growing bored.

But heart and mind have
no faucets—"Hot" and "cold,"
no switch for
"on" and "off."
Cannot one live
with concern,
read deeply,
and be still, relax?
Concern, undergirded
with confidence,
knowing that God
is in control.

January 15, 1976

Nothing More

Is there
somewhere, anywhere,
a little, lonesome cabin
lost among the forests,
on a wild, deserted shore;
an empty, waiting cabin:
rough-hewn, worn, and solid
with a dandy drawing chimney,
books, and windows, little more.
I'm tired of noise and traffic,
people pushing, phones and letters,
dates and deadlines, styles and headlines,
pride and pretense. I implore:
Find some solitary cabin,
near God's mountain masterpieces,
just a lost and lonesome cabin
where my tired soul can adore.

1976-77

The Murderer's Prayer

Beyond all custom
all tradition,
Lord, I would see
Your truth revealed;
then could I come,
in my condition,
to seek Your face,
and by Your grace
be healed.

But I confess
what You have known;
the hideous mess
my sins have grown,
coiling like some wild
and poisonous vine,
enmeshing other lives
with mine.

"Just as I am"
to me confirms
that none but You
accept such terms.

For only You
Who went the length
of Calvary
could know
the cost
of such forgiving love,
redeeming strength,
or show
Satan and his hordes
justice has been done.

While I
defeated by that cross
freed from
temptation's cords,
can glory in my loss,
for You have won!

And for all those
my sins have wounded
all along the way,
I plead Your freedom now;
for this I pray.

For L.M.
Cinnamon Hill, April 5, 1977

Father and Son

Sharp eyes he had, you say?
Yet I'll wager
they were filled with tears
many a day.
His heart watched, too,
for years;
and, busy as he was, he'd stand
filled with a yearning
for that son who'd left
for some far land,
spurning
love, and home, —and him;
frantic for fun, debating
all he had learned;
and so, the Father stood
    watching,
    yearning,
    waiting,
       for his son's returning.

Some might pity
his grieving.
Some might scoff.
True,
the Father watched him leaving
but, too,
He saw him coming back "when yet
a great way off."

1977

Not Finished

When we see
unsaintly "saints,"
(ourselves the guiltiest,
no doubt)
forgive us, Lord,
for our complaints;
and help us never
to forget,
whatever else, Lord,
You're about,
You have not finished
with us
—yet.

April 15, 1977

Left Out

Theirs was a moment
of glory brief.
I watched them pass
in their long black gowns
before the graduation crowd
swiftly, silently
some with relief
(you couldn't mistake it,
they all but sighed
when their diploma was passed
and they reached to take it).
And when together
they sat back down,
the applause was long,
commanding, loud;
parents, relatives,
friends looked on
and each in his own way
was proud.
But in the back, quiet, withdrawn,
I glimpsed the one
who didn't make it.

Montreat, May 8, 1977

And Forget

"Leave me with my dead:
I'd like to sit alone with him
just one more day," she said.
Memories of a time long gone,
so many crowded thoughts to think;
another life, another land,
and he the final link.

Efficient neighbors, all concern,
notified the funeral home. One
sent to get the borrowed bed
while she was out, but briefly gone,
arranging for her dead. "So when
she comes back home,"
one said
as she closed the door,
"all old reminders will be gone;
no strain, no fuss.
All will be as was before."

And so it was.

For H.S.
May 24, 1977

Relinquishment

I bring those whom I love
to You,
commit each to
Your loving care:
then carry them away again
nor leave them there:
forget that You
Who lived to die
(and rose again!)
care more than I.

So back I come
with my heart's weight,
confessing
my lack of faith
in You alone,
addressing
all I cannot understand
to You,
Who do.

You know each heart,
each hidden wound,
each scar,
each one who played a part
in making those
we bring to You
the ones they are
(and dearer each to You
than us, by far),

So now I give them
to Your loving care,
with thankful heart,
and leave them there.

May 29, 1977

Singing Through Thunder

He sang atop the old split rail
all while it thundered,
raindrops pelting him like hail,
and, I wondered:
How one small, vulnerable bird,
defying deafening thunder,
could make itself so sweetly heard.
And still I wonder.

Little Piney Cove
June 25, 1977

The Unseen Real

Above the clouds—
thick, boiling, low,
appeared the peaks
she came to know
as Father, Son,
and Holy Ghost.
Often when she
sought them most,
they would be hid,
in clouds, from view.

Distraught by cares,
she always knew,
silent, unseen,
they still were there
like God Himself—
unchanged, serene
and knowing this,
she gathered strength
for each day's journey,
length by length.

Montreux, July 16, 1977

Surprise

Such unorchestrated music
one has seldom heard:
dawn breeze
in the tops of trees,
liquid song of bird:
sparrow,
robin,
towhee,
indigo bunting,
wren,
meadow lark
and cardinal,
mockingbird,
finch,
and when
my soul is on tiptoe,
filled with ecstasy,
the turkey gobbles loudly
down by the locust tree!

Summer, 1977

Psalm 119:32

*E*nlarge my heart
to love You more,
when I am stumbling
on the way;
only the heart
enlarged by You
runs to obey.

L.P.C.
August 26, 1977

Forgive Their Sin

*"Forgive their sin—but if not blot me
out of the book you have written."
Exodus 32:32*

*I*f I could stand aside
and see
him walking through
those Splendor'd Gates
thrown wide,
instead of me . . .
If I could yield my place
to this him—my boy—
the tears upon
my upturned face
would be
of joy!

December 15, 1977

Lament

"Deep calleth unto deep . . ."

But there are no deeps in me,
O God,
nothing at all:
the babbling of a shallow brook,
puddles when the showers fall,
perhaps the edge of ocean shore . . .
no more.

December, 1977

In His Hands

"Sustaining all things . . ."
Hebrews 1:3

Listen, Lord,
a mother's praying
low and quiet:
listen, please.
Listen what her tears
are saying,
see her heart
upon its knees;
lift the load
from her bowed shoulders
till she sees
and understands,
You, Who hold
the worlds together,
hold her problems
in Your hands.

For d.c.
Cinnamon Hill, December 26, 1977

The Miles Between

The Far Country
may be near,
beneath this roof
or down the street;
yet he is there,
and I am here,
and when we meet,
those lonesome miles between
that can be felt
but never seen.

Jamaica, January 13, 1978

Sons

Mark 10:29,30

But what of
the ones
forsaken,
Lord, even for You?
The sons
now grown
who've never known
fathers who
had undertaken
to leave all
and follow You?
Some sons,
wounded beyond repair,
bitter, confused, lost,
these are the ones
for whom
mothers weep,
bringing them to You
in prayer
those nights they cannot sleep—
these, Lord,
are what it cost.

For T. and T.S.
January 15, 1978

Home and Heart

Lord,
in this frenzied puttering
around the house,
see more:
The dusting,
straightening,
muttering,
are all the poor
efforts of a heavy heart
to help time pass.
Praying on my knees
I get uptight;
for hearts and lives
are not the only things
that need to be
put right.

And, while I clean,
please,
if tears should fall,
they're settling the dust,
that's all.
Lord, I will straighten
all I can
and You—
take over what we mothers
cannot do.

January 19, 1978

My Flock

Proverbs 27:23

Like other shepherds
help me keep
watch o'er my flock by night;
mindful of each need,
each hurt, which might
lead one to stray,
each weakness
and each ill—
while others sleep
teach me to pray.
At night the wolves and leopards,
hungry and clever, prowl
in search of any wounded stray.
When they howl,
Lord, still
my anxious heart
to calm delight,
for the Great Shepherd
watches with me
over my flock
by night.

Little Piney Cove, January, 1978

New Lamb

Another lamb
will join the fold
tonight:
Good Shepherd
welcome her,
we pray,
and hold
her tight.

After Gigi called on her way to the hospital.
In the early morning Stephan called to say Jerusha had arrived.

Los Alamos, New Mexico, February 8, 1978

Wealthy

God's gracious gifts
of sun and sea,
of gentle weather,
come within reach
of each
whether
we are poor or rich.
Yet at times I wonder—
which is which?

Acapulco, February 27, 1978

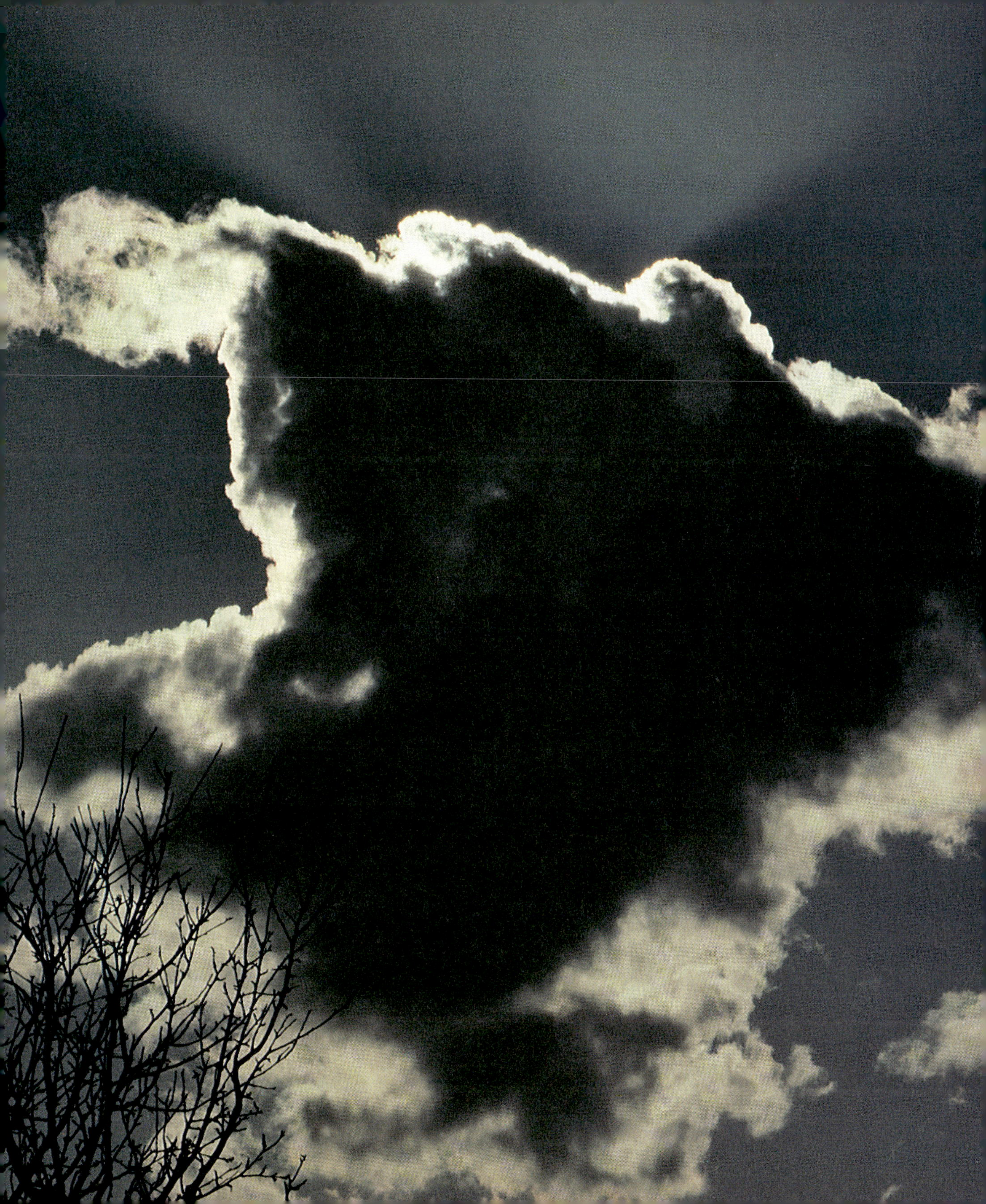

Hope

The long, gray winter
now is past—
the coldest we
have ever seen—
and I am glad
to note at last
earth's first bright
touch of green.

Milwaukee, March 22, 1978

A Glimpse of Glory

She was only one
in the crowd that day,
with a smile
(instead of words) to say:
Standing there
with cane and brace,
the light of heaven
on her face.

We didn't say a lot
(there was no time
for her to share her story),
yet I had got
a touch of special grace,
a glimpse of glory.

God had her carry
quite a heavy cross
for Him awhile;
and she, aware of all it cost,
was answering
with a smile.

April 4, 1978

Jesus in the Temple

He went
into the temple then,
casting out all who bought
and sold,
upsetting the seats
of those money men
trading the gifts of God
for gold.
And when
the outraged cries
had died,
and He stood alone
on that battlefield,
it was then
the blind and lame,
who gathered to Him there,
were healed.

Lord of our temple,
commandeered,
by alien interests,
let Your voice,
feared,
thunder with fury
through the whole,

Your whip be felt
on alien backs
till all have crept
away into the night.
My shambled soul,
now cleansed and still,
shall wait for You alone
to fill
it with Your love,
Your light.
And those in need
gather around to find
help for their lameness,
sight for eyes blind.

Second day of Passion Week, April 9, 1979

Primitive

I am a primitive.
   I love
primordial silences
   that reign
unbroken over ridge
   and plain,
unspoiled by
civilization's roar.
I love the lonesome sound
   of wind,
the solitary crashing
   of a tree,
the ceaseless wash of waves
   upon the shore,
wind, lightning, thunder,
   and the pouring rain
are symphonies to me.

1978

Lazarus

"Jesus wept."
But why?
knowing what lay ahead
moments away . . .
Was it because
He had not come,
had waited when He heard
Lazarus might die?
Lazarus was dead!
Was it in sympathy
with their raw grief,
their faith's
impotent lack?
Or could it be
because He
had to bring him
back?

1978

The Little Light

Leave a little light on
somewhere, in some room,
these dark, rainy days;
where, in the deepening gloom,
I, damped and grayed
by weather, might
in an unexpected place
glimpse warmth and cheer.
Those pragmatists who feel that light
is useful only,
have never known
the desolation dusk can bring,
or light's comforting sight,
when I am lonely.

Little Piney Cove
April 27, 1978

Flowers, Leaves

They come and go so quickly
Spring and Fall . . .
as if they had not really
come at all.
Perhaps
we could not take
too much of beauty,
breath-catching glory,
ecstasy without relief;
and so God made them
brief.

May 6, 1978

Crying

The unrelieved complaining
of the wind across the ridge,
rising of a sudden,
to a wild and lonesome roar,
like the sad, sustained resounding
of the surf upon some shore,
leaves my own heart strangely pounding:
—as if I'd heard God sighing
for a world astray and dying,
and somewhere, a lost soul crying,
wanting for more.

May 6, 1978
December 8, 1978 (spitting snow)
Christmas 1979 (snowing)

Tender

Lord, have Your way,
Be very tender Lord we pray
with one whose child
lies dead today.

Be tenderer, Lord, we plead
for those with runaways
for whom Moms bleed.

But tenderest of all with each
whose child no longer cares
is out of reach.

Memphis-Atlanta, May 14, 1978

Satan Speaks

Herein
lies my cleverest ploy,
hell's greatest power,
this plot
that fills me with Satanic joy:
convincing those within our
jurisdiction, that somehow
I am not.

May-June, 1978

Jeremiah 2:31

"Have I been a wilderness to you?"
   asked the Lord.
"A place of wandering
and of darkness
   as the night?"

No.
It is this void
in which I find myself.
This is my wilderness,
my place of wandering
in darkness and in fog.
You are light
and life.
All I long for,
all I need,
is You.

How can we walk together
once again?
How can I know You, Lord,
as I once knew?

And He,
through the echoing of my empty
heart,
replied,
"I shall be waiting for you
at the very spot
you left my side."

Paoli, July 15, 1978

Light for Darkness

Tonight
the lights went out,
(aftermath of a sudden storm)
trapped in the sudden dark
I groped about
to light the candles
and a fire
to keep me warm;
wondering how
men manage, who
have no fire, no candlelight
to company them
on some night of storm.

1978

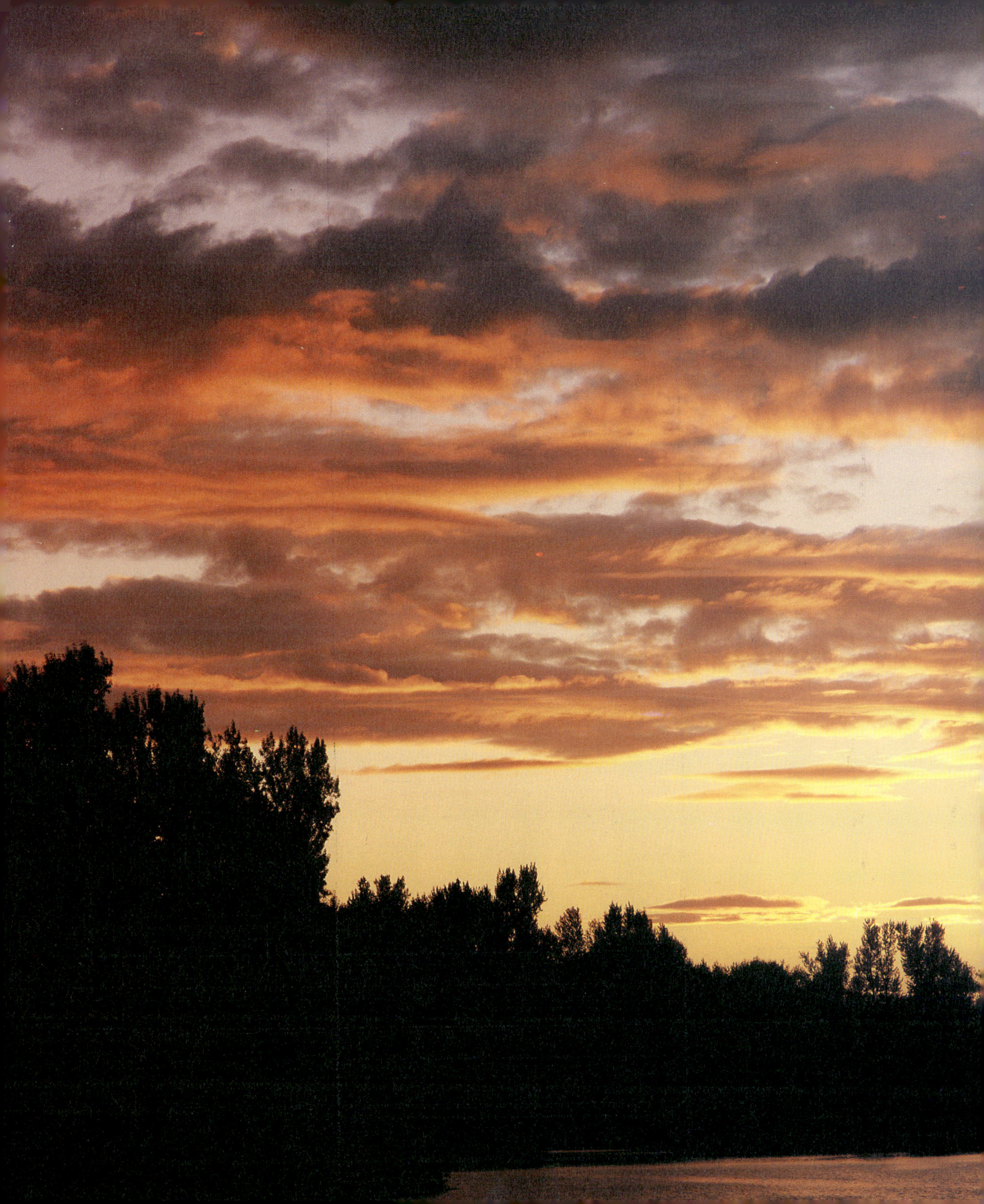

Cross-Bearing

He took His cross
as best He could
(cross-bearing was
so new to Him).
How could He tell
the torturous load
of rough-hewn wood
on that rutted road
where He was led,
would cut His shoulder
till it bled?
And then
He fell.

Of all the curious,
crowding round,
Who
stepping out, stooped down
to do
what Simon did
long years ago?
But He, Who
staggering beneath our cross
fell, too.

December 13, 1979

The Onward Look

Leave them quietly at His feet:
    Day is past;
Bitter mingled with the sweet,
    Dies are cast.
Reality surpassed the dreams,
    Kindly, He overruled my schemes;
His truth—those tentative "it seems"—
    Heaven at last!

January 1, 1980

Windshield Wipers

Blinking
back the tears
I'm thinking,
may just clear
the heart for sight;
as windshield wipers
help us
on a stormy,
windswept night.

March 18, 1980

What the Sea Longs For

If I lived within the churning
sound of sea's relentless yearning,
my soul would rise and fly to seek
what the sea longs for—unable to speak;
aware, as I go, of Him everywhere:
in my heart, in the clouds...the cold wet air...
And my soul would worship in joyful prayer,
receding as the waves recede,
returning with the waves' returning,
reaching up, as for Him, feeling,
then with the waves to kneeling...
                        to kneeling...
                                to kneeling.

May 7, 1980

For the Children

God of the Universe
in power abiding,
whose Son both death endured
and death defied,
returning omnipresent
as before; confiding
all–all to You,
an irrevocable trust,
I find my leaden spirit
rising from the dust.
Confident that You
Who've brought them
thus far on the way
will see them through.

May 29, 1977
June 29, 1980

White World

I awoke to a world
of whitening wonder:
all the bareness of
winter landscape under
soft white snow
falling...
and still falling
as the dusk falls.
The mountains 'round
are whited out,
and still it falls,
leaving only the nearer woods
etched stark against
the white about.
The only color I can see:
a red bird in a whitened tree.
The only sound in a world gone still:
a towhee on my windowsill.

Little Piney Cove, February 6, 1980

The Living, or the Dead?

Leave them to God
those distant, sinister souls
whose crimes unmentionable
stained history's pages red,
decimated races,
searing the minds of survivors;
leave them to God.
For there are those today
perpetrating crimes
as hideous as theirs;
unnoticed and unmentioned.
Only the past concerns.
What if, in satisfying vengeance,
we sacrifice the living for the dead?
Divert attention from the present
holocaust?
Why must more die
while those who could help
remain in mental ghettos
of a time long gone?
Perhaps some evil force
would have it so.
And still they die.
Diversionary tactics?
Is that why?

January 6, 1980
(after reading Life Magazine*)*

No Regrets

Let them go—
the things that have
accumulated through the years.
If they are only things
then go.
Let them go.
Like barnacles
they will impede the ship
and slow
it, when it should go
full speed ahead.
Why dread
the disentangling?
Does the snake
regret the shedding of its skin?
When the butterfly escapes
its chrysalis,
does regret
set in?

M.C.
June 10, 1980

Slave Collar

It hangs there
like an evil thing,
this curve of iron
that 'round some slave's neck
curled and snapped,
the slave, long past,
his collar worn rib-thin,
rigid in rust
as if at last
its own *rigor mortis*
had set in.

Little Piney Cove, September 20, 1978
Johnny Cash sent me an iron slave
collar which hangs above my desk.

Out of the Nest, and Back

The fledgling
eager to be free,
struggling
for liberty,
coming home
in later years,
found she came
in tears.

The other one,
nudged from the nest
(reluctantly,
to make her fly),
coming back
in later years,
found she could
not cry.

Tsingkiang, Kiangsu, China
May 14, 1980

Staff, and Rod

It is a fearful thing to fall
into Your hands, O living God![1]
Yet I must trust my all to You,
praying your staff and rod[2]
will comfort each in need
as well as break,
in love, the wayward leg. And yet I plead,
"Deal gently with the young man
for my sake."[3]

1 Hebrews 10:31
2 Psalm 23
3 2 Samuel 18:5

Little Piney Cove
August 3, 1980

Darkness into Light

Drifting, slipping, slow I went,
no leap in sudden haste,
but quietly I eased away
into this silent waste.

How long it's been, I do not know
(a minute from Him seems
like long nights of emptiness,
and silent screams).

I heard the distant promises,
wistful, and groped to see
a glimmer of Him in the dark:
Could He see me?

There was no pounding on the Gates,
no cry at Heaven's door;
I had no strength; my tears left
a puddle on the floor.

Then from my crumpled nothingness,
my dungeon of despair,
a quiet opening of the door—
a breath of Living Air.

He let me sleep, as if I'd died,
yet when the morning broke
the Risen Son discovered me,
and I awoke.

New I awoke; His warming love,
Updrawing, transformed everything.
Tell me—is this how an acorn feels
in Spring?

Little Piney Cove, August 30-September 1, October 10, 1980

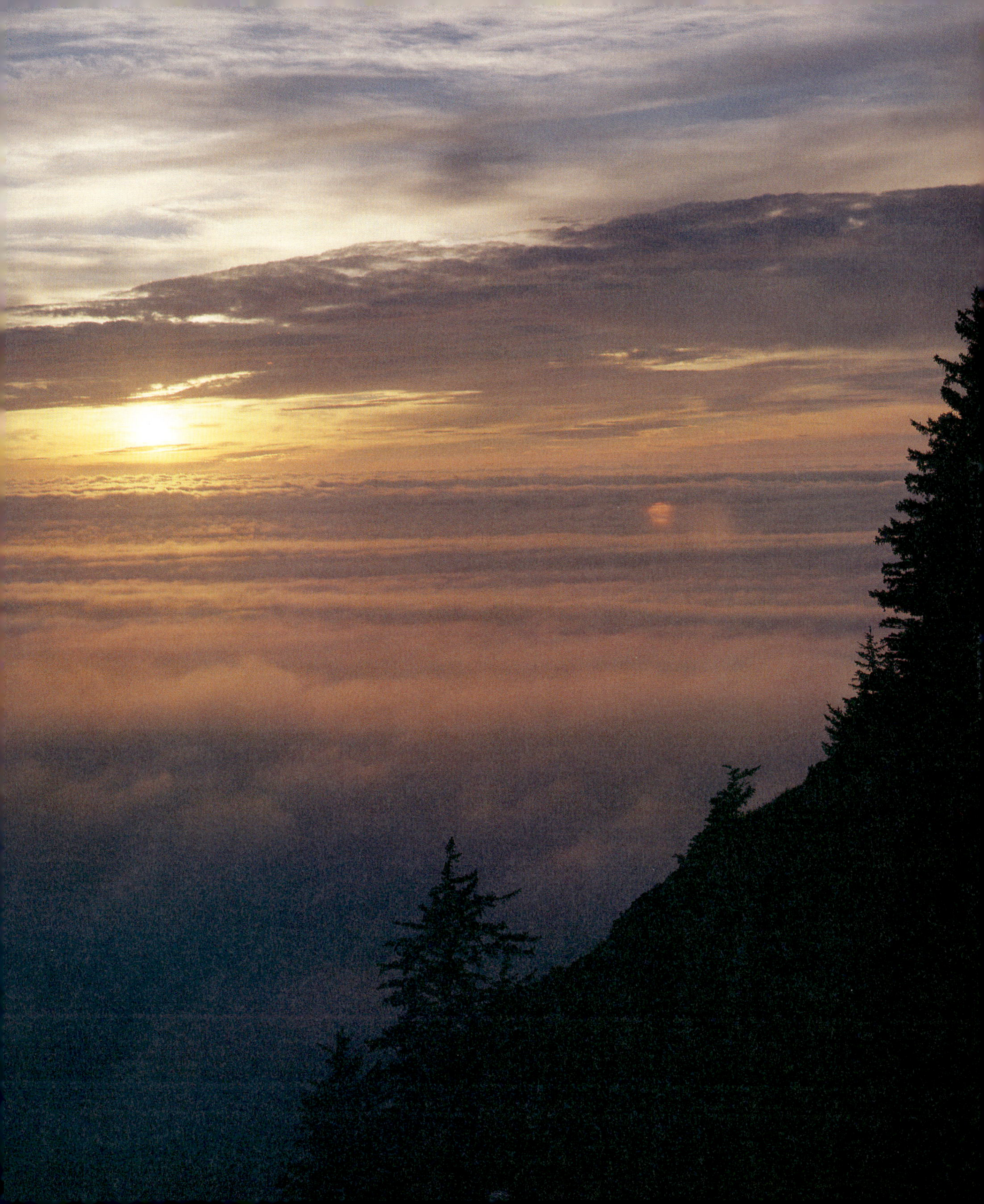

The Meaning of Wilderness

Moses' wanderings weren't
    all for naught:
Wandering, he learned the
    wilderness firsthand;
And later through this
    Devastation brought
His brothers from bondage to
    the Promised Land.

September 27, 1980

The Wrestling

Genesis 32:24-31

Lord, "With my Jacob," I would pray,
"wrestle until break of Day,"
till he, now knowing who Thou art,
tho' asked, will not let Thee depart;
saying "I will not let Thee free
unless Thou wilt first bless me."
O God of Jacob, who knew how
to change supplanters then, so now
deal, I pray, with this my son,
though he may limp when Thou art done.

October 5, 1980

My Jacob

*"Jacob was left alone, and a man
wrestled with him till daybreak"
Genesis 32:24*

He is my Jacob,
Lord,
and I must pray,
"wrestle with him,
please,
'till break of day."
My wrestling days are past
nor did they any good,
but if you'd take him on
I know it would.

In None of These

1 Kings 19:3-13

There has been wind
and earthquake, too;
followed by fire;
he stood, fear-thinned,
encaved, to view
the holocaust expire.

Yet, God, You were in none of these.
I listen for Your still, small voice—please.

Minneapolis, October 19, 1980

If Only

Hebrews 12:1

"Compassed about
with a great cloud . . ."
the Scriptures say;
If only I could hear,
one shout...
The distant roar
of that great crowd,
just some small word
    aloud . . .
    aloud . . .
to cheer my way.

Minneapolis, October 22, 1980

In This Fog

Sunk in this gray
depression
I cannot pray.
How can I give
expression
with no words
to say?
This mass of vague
foreboding
of aching care,
love with its
overloading
short-circuits prayer.
Then in this fog
of tiredness,
this nothingness, I find
a quiet, certain, knowing
that He is kind.

September, 1980

At Close of Day

God,
bless all young mothers
at end of day,
kneeling wearily with each
small one
to hear them pray.
Too tired to rise when done . . .
and yet, they do,
longing simply to sleep
one whole night through.

Too tired to sleep,
too tired to pray...
God,
bless all young mothers
at close of day.

Atlanta Airport, November 23, 1980

Two Sons

He had returned, the prodigal.
The father,
from his long months of waiting,
flew down the path
to welcome him once more,
killing the fatted calf,
calling for robes and ring
as if not anything
had gone between...all as before.
The celebration had begun.
Then a gloom fell—
It was the older son
who knew the younger well.
The Father stood between
the sinful "was,"
the righteous "might have been."

There are few
who know how a father's heart
can be torn in two.

December 22, 1980

God's Merriment

"God rest you merry,
gentlemen . . . "
and in these pressured days
I, too, would seek to be so blessed
by Him, who still conveys
His merriment, along with rest.
So I would beg, on tired knees,
"God rest me merry,
this Christmas, please . . . "

for R.B.G.
Christmas, 1980

Missing Her

This is her first Christmas
Home with You.
In our missing her, help us to view
things from her side:
the bliss of being There,
relatives to meet,
friends, and her brother, too.
And knowing that
her life here was complete,
not interrupted; give us grace
and free our hearts to face
whatever else it is You
have for us to do.

for Julie Codington
December 25, 1980

Escape?

"Where can I go from Your Spirit?"
Psalm 139:7-12

Fleeing from You,
nothing he sees
of Your preceding
as he flees.

Choosing his own path
how could he know
Your hand directs
where he shall go.

Thinking he's free,
"free at last,"
unaware Your right hand
holds him fast.

Waiting for darkness
to hide in night,
not knowing, with You
the dark is as light.

Poor prodigal!
Seeking a "where" from "whence"
how does one escape
omnipotence?

for R.B.G.

Close to You

Cradle her within your arms
when evening falls
after the wearying day;
secure her in tenderness
that she may sleep
her tiredness away.
 Passion is a gift from God,
 but when the body aches
 with weariness, one longs
for quiet love. It takes
so little to restore the soul,
so little to renew:
just gather her within your arms,
let her sleep close to you.

1980

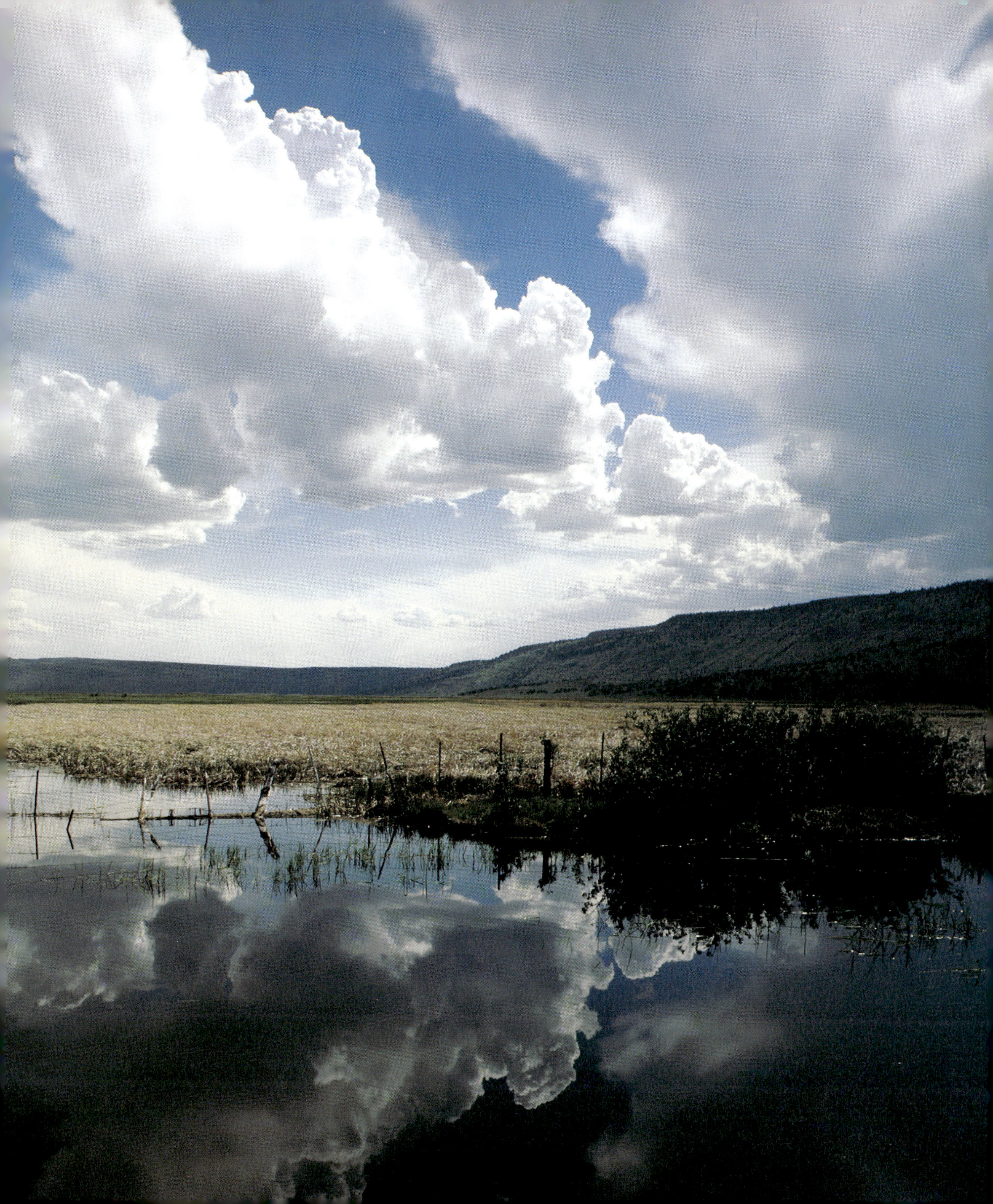

A Tree

He fell on the sidewalk.
I saw him fall,
too drunk to walk
he could only crawl
to a scraggly tree
that grew near the street;
with the help of that tree
he got on his feet.
In my heart always,
God, help me see
he got on his feet
for...
there was a tree!

Mexico, March, 1981

Heading Home

The harbor:
loaded freighters,
cruisers, yachts, and ferries.
Yet,
as the lights
twinkle on, one by one,
in the quickening dusk,
my heart is with
that one small sailboat
heading home.

Mexico, February, 1981

He Whom Thou Lovest

God,
he whom Thou lovest
is ill,
and it is night.
Numb we wait
Thy will,
helpless with fright.

(How can mere hours be
an eternity?)

Slowly we know
before a word
is said:
Lord,
he whom Thou lovest
is dead.

November 27, 1981

Sleep

He's not dead,
but we
struggling to live
upon this cursed earth:
wearied by work,
not free,
to come and go at will
bound by gravity,
the limits of
our mortality.

Since he has broken through
the limitations of this life,
entered There
eternally young, and free
from sin and sickness,
aging, and the woe
that cramp and cripple us—
God, who are we
to mourn and weep
when it is not he,
but we,
who are asleep?

November 28, 1981

Homing

Psalm 116:15

The eager parents wait
the homing of their child
from far lands desolate,
from living wild;
wounded and wounding along the way,
their sorrow for sin ignored,
from stain and strain of night and day
to home, assured.

So the Heavenly Father waits
the homing of His child;
throwing wide those Heavenly Gates
in glorious welcome wild!
His, His the joy by right,
(once crucified, reviled),
So—precious in God's sight
is the death of His child.

For Velma
Friday, November 2, 1984

Prayed For

Please—
don't feel condemned.
It happened quickly
and you were not prepared
for new defiance,
deceit honed to perfection,
     cunning—a science
     daring detection.
     And you who cared before,
now, if possible
care even more.
Somewhere the straying one
is out there hurt and hiding,
running and groping,
afraid he'll be found
yet somehow, hoping;
a composite of all God's strays.

All who share
His love
stand with you nights and days
in prayer.

While up above
He who went the length of Calvary
to get us back, prays too.

So, when the load
is more than you can bear,
remember you are prayed for
both here,
—and There.

No Room

"No Room for Him . . ."
Somewhere behind the crackle of the
fire,
the music of each old loved Christmas
hymn,
the rush of buying gifts,
the tall green tree to trim,
the maddening crowd of Christmas joys
families, food, enchanting toys.
The day explodes in cheer,
wears on in companionship
and laughter.
Our cup's filled to the brim.
Then dusk, and after
the long day's crush
in that exhausted hush
before sleep,
we know that once again we've
made
"no room for Him."

January 13, 1980

Silent

Zephaniah 3:17, marginal note

He will be silent
in His love . . . "
and I
who looked for words to prove
His love and care
(that He is
and He is there)
now know
in all this silence
blank and grim,
this throbbing quiet,
this aching void—
I am so
loved
by Him.

August 29, 1977

Question

*P*eace
came as suddenly today
as the storm came
a day ago.
My soul was drenched
in wind and rain
frozen in fear
that fell like snow.
Then all was still.
Had someone prayed?
I do not know.

for Ned
January 19, 20, 1977

In Need

He knew the pressure of the crowds
curious, to see Him do
some miracle.
Yet when, in need, one touched His robe
He knew.

In my small way, though I am pressured, too,
may I be sensitive to feel
and tell
the difference between pretended needs
and real.

Tampa, March 17, 1979
Enroute to Paris, March 19, 1980

Lovely Saturday

There is no one left to walk with now
No small, warm hand within my own
And woods are less enchanting
When explored alone.

March 29, 1980

Thirsty

"All my springs are in Thee"
Psalm 87:7 (Book of Common Prayer)

She craved for love
and tried to satisfy her thirst
with things. With things
He blessed her
(or so she thought at first).
But substitution only brings
a deeper thirst,
as when a man, adrift at sea,
sun-bleached and wind-parched, craves
to quench his thirst with salty waves
only to find his last state even worse.
So, surfeited, unsatisfied, not greed
but thirst drove her to gather more
than met her need.
Ignoring Love's fresh springs
even more thirsty than before,
at last she knew that she'd
become a prisoner of things.

Little Piney Cove, May 21, 1977

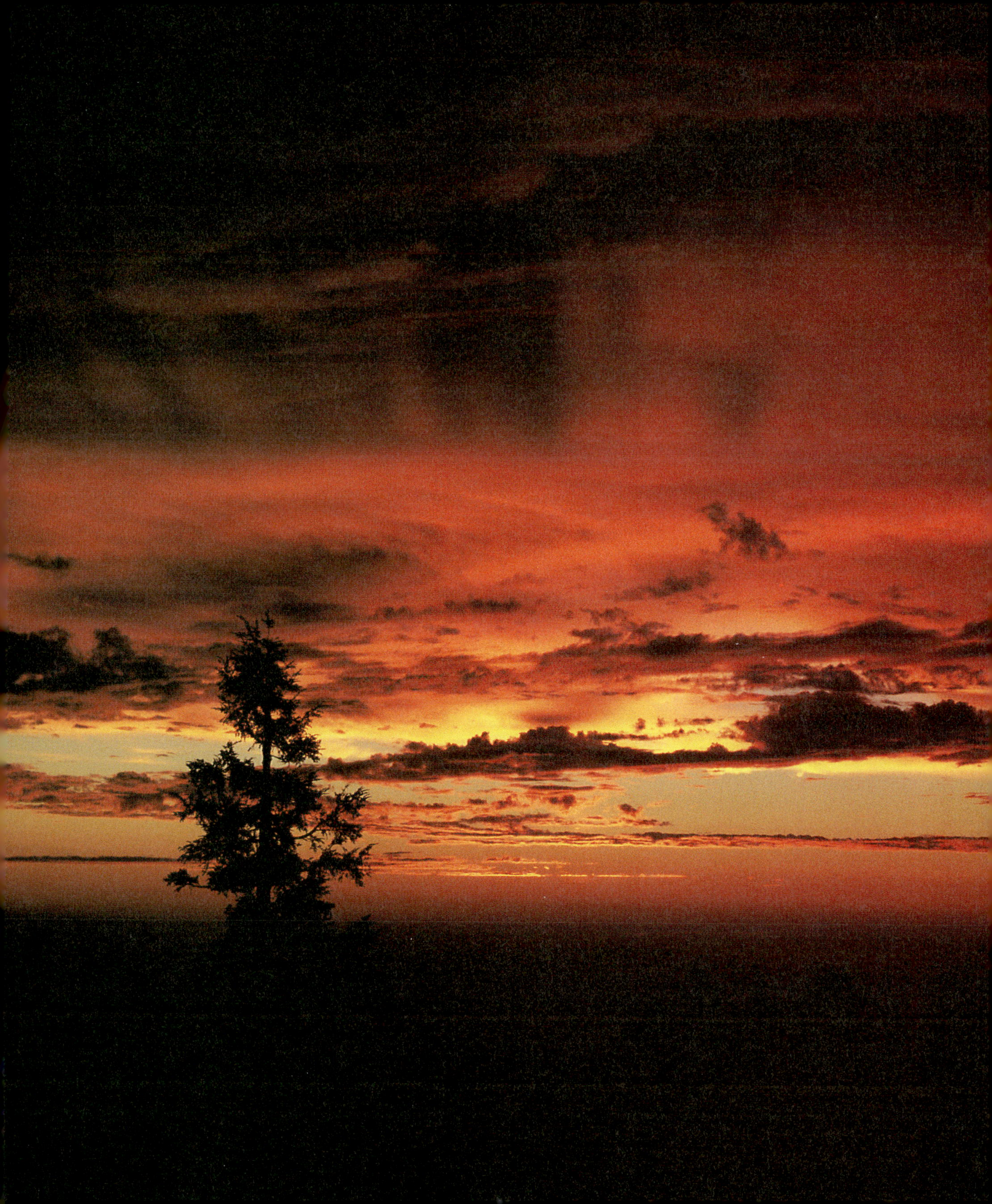

Substitute

To kill with words,
without regret—
a cruel thing
he knows is;
then thinking
flowers
will resurrect
he sends her
twelve red roses.

His Way

As I was praying
day and night,
night and day,
quietly God was saying
"Let there be light,"—
My way.

Song

Sing it clear
and softly,
sing it quiet
and low—
Jesus died for sinners
long, long ago.

Sing it soft
and clearly,
low and quiet, too
Jesus died for sinners
Jesus died for you.

Lift your head
and sing it
sing for all to hear—
Jesus loves each sinner,
loves each, far and near.

Voice from the Dead

"He saved others," sneered the crowd,
"Himself He cannot save."
True, how true! Shout it aloud,
Aloud...from an empty grave!

Easter Sunday, Little Piney Cove, April 11, 1982

Forsaking All

A fortune or a fishnet,
when we hear Him call,
He doesn't say "how much" and yet
His "all" means *"all."*

Then, and Now

The house was full of living then
And there was need to view
the quiet contours of the hills,
heaven's vast expanse of blue.

This old house is empty now,
with mostly only me,
the trees are crowding up the hill
as if for company.

I would not have them back for good—
my birds have learned to fly—
but I find lovely comfort when
a wild bird nests close by.

Candlelight

Oddly, in
this room tonight—
strange place—
strange town—
twilight—
yet here, alone,
I feel at home
a small fire cheers
my lonely night,
a tiny fire
called candlelight.

Jamaica, January 13, 1978

Home Address

My home address?
Christ!
In Him I dwell
wherever else I be—
as bird in the air,
as branch in the vine,
as tree in the soil,
as fish in the sea.
He is my home.

My business address?
Here:
Little Piney Cove
or London, Corinth,
Calcutta or Rome,
Shanghai or Paris.
My business address?
Wherever He puts me—
But He is my home.

The Last Word

God held me
in His silence—
stilled
by the knowing
of His love,
I heard
the rolling
of the thunder
death
    tolling...
        tolling...
           tolling...
under
the darkening sky
I saw and see,
I heard and hear,
the tragic be
proof, He is near—
Waiting...waiting...
To be seen
and heard.
He who is
and has been
has
the last word.

Peking, June, 1989

Tiananmen Square

A still day—
the sky grew dark,
(darkness fell, too,
at Calvary)
thunder, like the wrath of God,
shook the earth
as lightning split
low-hung clouds;
then came the rain.
Pelting the crowds
walking
thronging
laughing
longing—
It was still dark
the sky grew black. Thunder
came from tanks and guns:
a generation fell under
mindless wrath. Lightning split
power from people.
Brute force hit.
Then came the wind and rains.

To wash away
the stains?

Beijing, May-June, 1989

Golgotha

The darkness fell
too soon that day.
It was still day
when darkness fell
the rolling
thunder, like a knell
of some grim bell
tolling
for the dead.

What dead?
For all of life
lay ahead.

In His Silence

Gently
God held me
in His silence;
stilled
by the knowing
of His love.

The sky was dark
Yet it was day.
The lowering clouds
were torn asunder,
the lightning streaked
in fury
I heard the rolling
of the thunder,
like a knolling
for the dead.
It flashed
and rolled again—
again.

Then came the rain
not gently
but in driven sheets.
Across the city, lanes
and streets.
And it was night.
Night.

Gently
God held me
in His silence,
stilled
by the knowing
of His love.

Beijing, May 17, 1989

First Line Index

A burst of song	36
A fortune or a fishnet,	131
A house	45
A still day—	136
Above the clouds—	57
Another lamb	67
As I was praying	128
Beyond all custom	48
Blinking	87
But there are no deeps in me,	61
But what of	64
Compassed about	103
Cradle her within your arms	110
Dear Lord,	24
Dear one,	18
"Death, be not long.	38
Drifting, slipping, slow I went,	96
Dusty my soul tonight.	8
Enlarge my heart	59
Fleeing from You,	109
Gently	138
God held me	135
God of the Universe	89
God rest you merry,	107
God's gracious gifts	68
God,	115
God, bless all young mothers	105
God, make me worthy to be his wife:	15
Have I been a wilderness to you?,	81
He died—	32
He does not go alone	44
He fell on the sidewalk:	113
He had returned, the prodigal.	106
He is my Jacob	101
He knew the pressure of the crowds	122
He sang atop the old split rail	54
He saved others," sneered the crowd,	130
He took His cross	85
He went	73
He will be silent	120
He's not dead,	116
Herein	80
I am a primitive.	74
I awoke to a world	90
I bring those whom I love	53
I'll be a bride—	19
If I could stand aside	60
If I lived within the churning	88
If I were stranded	37
Inasmuch" a cup of water,	2
Is there	47
It hangs there	93
It is fearful thing to fall	95
It isn't your gold or silver,	1
It was so very good of God	16
Jesus wept."	75
Larger than life	35
Leave a little light on	76
Leave me with my dead:	52
Leave them quietly at His feet:	86

Leave them to God	91
Let them go—	92
Like a shadow declining,	5
Like other shepherds	66
Listen, Lord,	62
Lord Jesus, take this life of mine,	4
Lord,	65
Lord, have Your way,	79
Lord, let mine be	17
Lord, With my Jacob," I would pray,	100
low gray skies,	34
Manicured, styled,	39
May I so live,	43
Moses' wanderings weren't	99
My home address?	134
No Room for Him . . .	119
Now that I love you	23
Now unto Him Who is able	3
Oddly, in	133
Ours is a little home	22
Peace	121
Please, God,	21
Please	118
Puppet,	26
Sharp eyes he had, you say?	49
She craved for love	124
She was only one	72
Sing it clear	129
So helpless a thing my heart	10
Spare not the pain	6
Such unorchestrated music	58
Sunk in this gray	104
The darkness fell	137
The eager parents wait	117
The Far Country	63
The harbor:	114
The house was full of living then	132
The long, gray winter	71
The Lord shall fight for you, and you	9
The night	30
The sin-scarred	20
The unrelieved complaining	78
Theirs was a moment	51
There are so many thoughts on love	12
There has been wind	102
There is no one left to walk with now	123
They come and go so quickly	77
They say	46
This is her first Christmas	108
This is the day	33
To kill with words,	127
Tonight	82
Turbulent ocean	29
We bought this cove	25
When we come to know Jesus as Savior	7
When we see	50
White flowers	40
You held my hand	11

Design by Brenda Josee and Bruce DeRoos
Photographs by Steve Terrill

CLOUDS ARE THE DUST OF HIS FEET
© 1992 by Ruth Bell Graham

Published by Crossway Books,
a division of Good News Publishers,
1300 Crescent Street,
Wheaton, Illinois 60187.

Printed in the United States of America.

All rights reserved. No part of this publication may be reproduced, stored in a retrieval system, or transmitted, in any form or by any means, electronic, mechanical, photocopying, recording, or otherwise, without the prior written permission of the publisher.

Library of Congress Cataloging-in-Publication Data

Graham. Ruth Bell.
    Clouds are the dust of his feet/Ruth Bell Graham.
      p.   cm.
    ISBN 0-89107-707-3 : $24.95
     1. Christian poetry, American. I. Title.
PS8557.R222C58 1992
811'.54—dc20   92-26883
                                                     CIP

93 94 95 96 97 98 99 - 10 9 8 7 6 5 4 3 2